Prairie Girl's Song

Lyrics by **Kate Ferris**
Illustrations by **Mary Ann Tully**

To hear **Kate Ferris** sing
"Prairie Girl's Song", go to **www.kateferris.ca**

Prairie Girl's Farm

wetland

sunflowers

fiel

clover

2

flax field

Burr Oak
with swing

natural
prairie

farm house

flicker
tree

fairy
tree

garden

pond

willows

3

gravel road

Blackbird sittin' on a barb-wire fence singin' to the mornin',

4

he sings so loud and clear,
to let us know summer days are here.

Bullfrog croakin' in a cat-tail pond
dragonflies are swarmin',

6

as if they want to play,
just another beautiful Prairie day!

Clouds go rollin' through a sky so blue
windblown grasses wavin',

8

the willows dance and bend,
while a Monarch lights on a milkweed stem.

Tire swing hangin' from an old oak tree
bare feet set it swayin',

the scent of new-mown hay,
just another beautiful Prairie day!

Sunflowers wavin' in a field of gold
sea of flax beside 'em,

12

purple clover lines the gravel road,
makes you want to go out a-ridin'.

13

15

*Cricket chirpin' by the old screen door
woodpecker's a-drummin',*

18

horned owl hootin' from an old pine tree,
to let us know night time's a-comin'.

'Neath the yellow of the back porch light
spider's busy spinnin',

she'll work the whole night through,
her web will sparkle with mornin' dew.

Fireflies sprinkled on a dew-damp lawn
here and there they're glowin',

22

they shine with fairy light,
just another beautiful Prairie night.

23

Wishin' star in an ink-black sky
crescent moon's a-grinnin',

24

it's such a pretty sight,
just another beautiful Prairie night.

25

It's such a pretty sight,
just another beautiful Prairie night.

Prairie Girl's Song

Words and Music by Kate Ferris

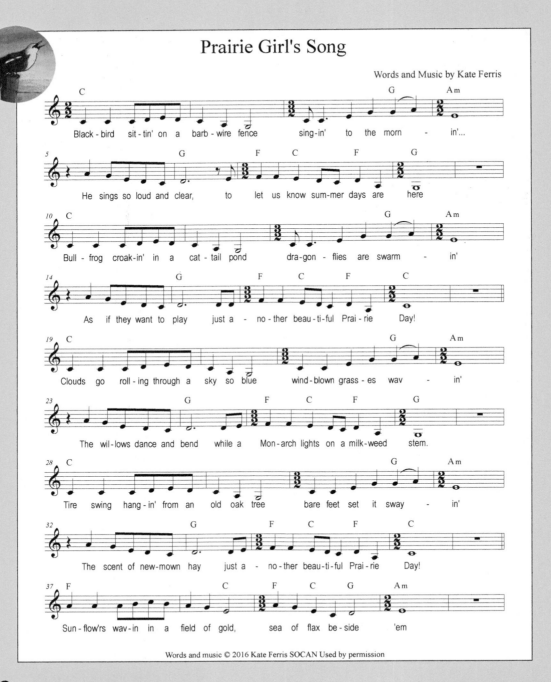

Black - bird sit - tin' on a barb - wire fence sing - in' to the morn - in'...

He sings so loud and clear, to let us know sum - mer days are here

Bull - frog croak - in' in a cat - tail pond dra - gon - flies are swarm - in'

As if they want to play just a - no - ther beau - ti - ful Prai - rie Day!

Clouds go roll - ing through a sky so blue wind - blown grass - es wav - in'

The wil - lows dance and bend while a Mon - arch lights on a milk - weed stem.

Tire swing hang - in' from an old oak tree bare feet set it sway - in'

The scent of new - mown hay just a - no - ther beau - ti - ful Prai - rie Day!

Sun - flow'rs wav - in in a field of gold, sea of flax be - side 'em

Prairie Girl's Song

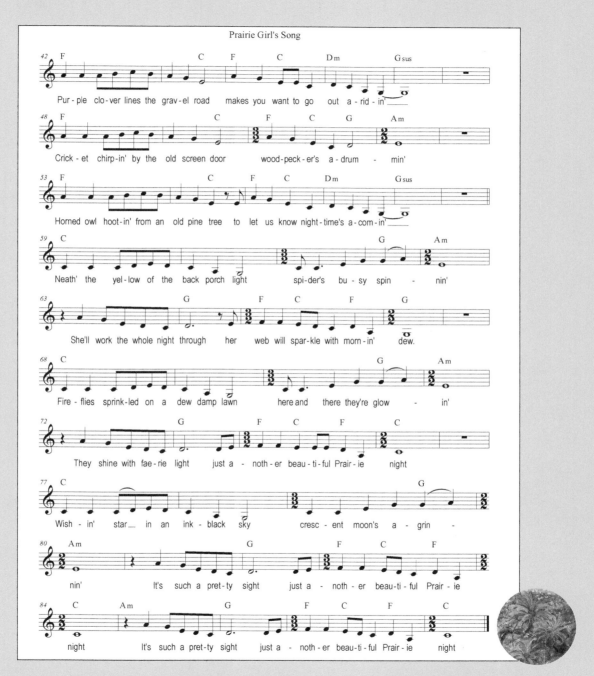

Prairie Plants and Animals Found in "Prairie Girl's Song"

Silverleaf Psoralea (front cover) These wildflowers are also called "Prairie Tumbleweed" since they tumble across the prairie when the wind blows. They look silvery because they have white hairs covering their stems and leaves. The silver colour reflects the sun's light, helping the plant stay cool and retain moisture.

Black-eyed Susans (front cover, pages 14, 26) Black-eyed susans are prairie wildflowers in the sunflower family. They attract butterflies. They were used by some First Nations peoples as a medicine plant to treat colds, flu, and snake bites.

Magpie (front cover, page 9) Magpies have a keen sense of smell to find dead animals to eat. They are one of the most intelligent birds. They are very noisy. Their calls include a whining "MAG" sound and a series of loud, harsh "CHUCK" notes.

Monarch Butterfly (front cover, page 8, back cover) By eating poisonous milkweed plants, monarch butterflies become poisonous too, and cannot be eaten by other animals. They migrate in large groups to Mexico for the winter.

Canada Goose (page 2) Canada geese make a deep, musical "HONK-HONK." They migrate in a "V" formation, up to nine km high. They stop to feed on seeds and plants in wetlands, grasslands or cultivated fields. Adults can live to twenty-four years old.

Northern Harrier (pages 3 - male, 15 - female) Northern harriers perch low in trees and fly close to the ground with wings raised as they use their sense of hearing to search for birds, mice, frogs, and other prey. Males and females look very different.

Echinacea or Purple Coneflower (page 4) Echinacea is a prairie wild-flower. Its long roots were used by some First Nations peoples as a pain-killer for toothaches and sore throats. Some people buy cold medicine made from echinacea.

Gaillardia (pages 4, 14, 26) Gaillardia are a prairie wildflower used as food by caterpillars. They are called "Indian blanket flower" as the petal colours look like the patterns on blankets made by First Nations peoples in the southwest United States.

Yellow-headed Blackbird (pages 4, 5, 26, back cover) Yellow-headed blackbirds like freshwater marshes and often look for food in nearby farmlands. The adult females are dusky brown, with no wing patch, but with white streaks on the breast.

Sharp-tailed Grouse (page 5) Sharp-tailed grouse males inflate their purple neck sacs, rattle their wing quills and utter loud booming calls when dancing for mates. They eat grasshoppers, berries, grains, buds, leaves, and flowers.

Pelican (page 6) Pelicans are one of the largest water birds. The whole flock may work together to catch fish by "herding" them into shallow water, then scooping the fish out of the water into their throat pouches that can hold thirteen litres of water.

Dragonfly (pages 6, 7) Dragonflies are important mosquito-eating insects. When they land, they hold their four wings out to their sides. Humans destroy their wetland habitats, so if there are lots of dragonflies, it means that their wetland is healthy.

Bullfrog (page 6) Bullfrogs are the largest frog in North America. They make very loud bass notes which sound like "JUG-O'-RUM" and can be heard for 500 metres! Their populations are low, so it is very important not to remove them from their ponds.

Cattails (pages 6, 7) Cattails are tall marsh plants which grow in thick stands. Their brown "heads" are made of tightly packed female flowers which become seeds and a thin "tail" of paler male flowers above, which disappear early in the season.

Western Painted Turtle (page 7) These are the largest of the painted turtles. They have one of the most intricate colour patterns of all turtles. They eat aquatic vegetation, insects, crayfish, and small mollusks (snails). They like to bask in the sun.

Great Blue Heron (page 7) Great blues are the largest North American herons. When they fly, their necks are folded back into an "S" shape and their long legs trail out behind. They feed by standing still in the water for long periods of time and, "in a flash like lightning," grabbing fish and other animals with their sharp bills.

Milkweed (page 8) After they flower, milkweeds produce bumpy seed-pods which burst open to let out hundreds of fluffy seeds that float on the breeze. They are important plants because monarch butterflies and many other insects eat them.

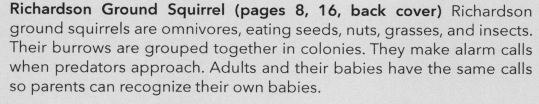

Richardson Ground Squirrel (pages 8, 16, back cover) Richardson ground squirrels are omnivores, eating seeds, nuts, grasses, and insects. Their burrows are grouped together in colonies. They make alarm calls when predators approach. Adults and their babies have the same calls so parents can recognize their own babies.

Peach Leaf Willows (page 9) Peach leaf willows are a native tree which is common beside creeks. Each tree has either male or female flowers, pollinated by insects. Their flowers secrete sweet nectar to attract insects, so they are good for bees.

Burr Oak (page 10) Burr oaks are a type of white oak; they have the largest range of any oak. Their early leaves are yellow and they have the biggest acorns of all the American oak trees. Their wood is used for furniture, flooring, boats, and barrels.

Sandhill Cranes (page 11) Sandhill cranes roost for the night in groups, standing together in shallow water. To attract a mate in spring, they leap two metres into the air with wings half spread, calling loudly. They walk great distances for food.

Tiger Swallowtail Butterfly (page 12) Tiger swallowtails feed on manure, dead animals, and flower nectar using their long tongues. They have "tails" on their hind wings that look like the tails of swallows. Their wingspan is up to ten centimetres.

Sharp-shinned Hawk (page 13) These hawks get their name from their long slender bodies and tails. The female is larger than the male. They eat mostly small birds, mammals, bats, reptiles, grasshoppers, and larger insects.

Wild Bergamot (page 15) Wild bergamot is a prairie wildflower which is a member of the mint family. It has a square stem and a pleasant smell. It can be used to make tea. Some First Nations peoples used it to treat colds, the flu, and infections.

Thirteen-lined Ground Squirrel (page 15) Thirteen-lined ground squirrels live in open areas with short grass, such as lawns, golf courses, and pastures. They eat leaves, roots, insects, corn, and wheat. They greet each other by touching noses and lips.

Mallard Duck (page 16) Mallard ducks are the best-known wild duck. The male has a glossy green head. They are one of the first ducks to arrive back in spring. They are surface feeders or "dabblers," so are often seen tipped up, tail in the air.

Burrowing Owl (page 16) Burrowing owls are endangered because most grassland habitat has become farmland. It is the only owl that nests in the ground using burrows of badgers, foxes or ground squirrels. One family eats 1800 rodents in summer.

Red Fox (page 17) Not all red foxes are red. Other colours are brown, black, and silver (even in the same litter). They eat voles, mice, hares, and rabbits. They have a litter of one to ten pups between March and May every year.

Field Cricket (page 18) Crickets feed by night and eat insects and plants. They have loud chirping or trilling "songs" to attract a mate. People are now eating crickets, either roasted or ground into flour, as they are an excellent source of protein!

Northern Red-shafted Flicker (page 19) Flickers, more than any other woodpeckers, spend lots of their time on the ground looking for ants to eat. One study revealed 3000 ants in one flicker's stomach! They fly with a wave-like, up-and-down pattern.

Great Horned Owl (pages 19, 24) Great horned owls nest in trees, caves or on the ground. They are mainly nocturnal and eat small birds and mammals, like mice and large prey, like skunks and grouse. Their call is a series of three to eight loud hoots.

Cecropia Moth (page 20) Cecropias are Canada's largest moths; members of the giant silk moth family. Adults do not eat and live for only two weeks. Females emit pheromones, chemicals which the males' antennae can detect from two km away.

White-tailed Deer (page 22) These are the largest deer in North America. They wave their tails like white flags when they run. They live in forests, swamps, and brushy areas. They are browsers, eating twigs, shrubs, fungi, acorns, and grass.

Badger (page 22) Badgers are most active at night when they hunt for ground squirrels, mice, snakes, and insects. They have long, strong claws which they use for digging their burrows and for digging prey out of burrows.

Black-footed Ferret (page 24) Black-footed ferrets are one of the most endangered mammals and the only ferret native to North America. They nest in prairie dog burrows and eat prairie dogs, rabbits, birds, and ground squirrels.

Constellation Aquila (page 24) Aquila is said to be the eagle that held the thunderbolts of Zeus, King of the gods, until he needed them. The brightest star in Aquila is Altair, which is one corner of the "Summer Triangle" of bright summer stars.

Constellation Sagittarius (page 25) Sagittarius is a constellation that looks, to us, like a teapot. The ancient Greeks thought that it looked like a centaur (half man, half horse) with a bow and arrow aiming toward Scorpius.

Constellation Scorpius (page 25) Scorpius or Scorpio is a group of stars in the shape of a scorpion. The scorpion is supposed to have killed Orion, the hunter, with its sting. Scorpius rises in the sky as Orion sets. It contains the bright star Antares.

Coyote (page 25) Coyotes are members of the dog family. They are most active at night, looking for rodents, rabbits, songbirds, and deer. Their family is made up of a dominant mated pair and other members who help feed the pups.

Northern Long-eared Bat (page 25) These bats are endangered because of white-nose syndrome, a fungus which is killing bats. They have only one pup each year and live in the boreal forest, hibernating in caves, rock crevasses or under bark.

About the Author

Kate Ferris is a singer, songwriter, storyteller and music educator who grew up on a farm near Holland, Manitoba and enjoyed a 'free range' childhood. Her love of the Prairie finds its way into many of her songs. Kate and her husband, luthier Fred Casey, live in Manitoba's Interlake where they appreciate the sights and sounds of rural life. She is thrilled to have her words translated into the beautiful artwork created by her dear friend Mary Ann Tully. *"Prairie Girl's Song"* is dedicated to Kate's niece, Karen Ferris, who grew up on the very same farm, dreamed in the very same bedroom, and who - regardless of where she may live - will always be a Prairie Girl.

Go to Kate Ferris' website (www.kateferris.ca) to hear Kate singing *"Prairie Girl's Song"*.

About the Illustrator

Mary Ann Tully is an artist and teacher who loves sharing art and picture books with children. Her art studio in a log home called "Wenrio" (a Huron word meaning "in a grove of cedars") is located in a magical forest in rural southern Ontario. Mary Ann's appreciation of prairie ecology was fostered through living in Manitoba for six years and visiting the prairies on many occasions. She and musician Kate Ferris have been friends since teaching together in Thompson, Manitoba. *"Prairie Girl's Song"* is the result of their shared dream to create a children's book together.

Visit Mary Ann Tully's website (www.maryanntully.net) to see more images of her art.

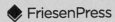

FriesenPress

Suite 300 - 990 Fort St
Victoria, BC, V8V 3K2
Canada

www.friesenpress.com

ISBN
978-1-4602-9461-1 (Hardcover)
978-1-4602-9462-8 (Paperback)
978-1-4602-9463-5 (eBook)

1. JUVENILE NONFICTION, MUSIC, SONGBOOKS

Distributed to the trade by The Ingram Book Company